ISBN 978-0-483-14386-9
PIBN 10500852

The University of California Magazine

VOLUME VII   SEPTEMBER, 1901   No. 5

JOSEPH LE CONTE.

THE MEASURE OF OUR LOVE FOR HIM.

BY WM. E. RITTER

He is gone beyond the reach of our voices.
A mysterious love that until now we did not know
We would tell him but cannot.
Tell him! Love that bindeth beyond the grave is not told!
Such love tilleth into rich fruitage
The seeds of his immortality to whom it goeth out—
Seeds planted by his own hand
In the eager soil of other lives—
          And so uttereth itself.

THE GREATNESS OF JOSEPH LE CONTE.

BY THOMAS R. BACON.

WHEN the news came to us that he, whom we all loved, the great teacher and good man, had passed from "the utmost bound of the everlasting hills" he loved so well into the immediate presence of the eternal verities in which he had already so largely lived, no one could feel a real regret that so fitting a life was so fittingly ended. The history of the University of California has not been an untroubled one. There have been times of tumult and dispute. But across it

all there runs one straight, shining line of white, the path un-
swervingly trodden out by the blameless feet of Joseph Le
Conte.   He had the power of inspiring reverence and affection even in those who scarcely knew him.   Men had only to
enter into the sphere of his transmuting influence to love him,
and to be better for that love.   His mere presence was peace.
The "good gray head which all men knew" was a luminary
with healing in its radiance, a radiance which transfigured
those upon whom it fell.   Why there was such saving power
in the man, it is not hard to tell.   His great knowledge was
added to the simplicity that is found in the heart of a child.
He was one of the pure in heart, who see God.   He was a
great scientist, he was a great philosopher, but we know that
he was greater in another way,—he kept unsoiled, unstained,
that little part of the life of God which came to him at his
birth, and with the faith of a little child he walked, unspot-
ted, from the world.

The apparent chasm between his traditional faith and the
discoveries of modern science interested him greatly, but
troubled him not at all.   For the help of those who were
troubled thus, he sought to impart to others what was his
own clear vision of these things.   What Longfellow said of
another great geologist might well have been spoken concerning him:

> And Nature, the old nurse, took
>   The child upon her knee,
> Saying, "Here is a story-book
> .   Thy father has written for thee."
>
> "Come, wander with me," she said,
>   "Into regions yet untrod,
> And read what is still unread
>   In the manuscript of God."
>
> And he wandered away and away
>   With Nature, the dear old nurse,
> Who sang to him night and day
>   The rhymes of the universe.

And whenever the way seemed long,
  And his strength began to fail,
She would sing a more wonderful song,
  Or tell a more wonderful tale.

So she keeps him still a child
  And will not let him go:—

but she had to let him go at last. The Father himself stooped
down and took the child from the nurse's arms. And now
we sorrow most of all for this, that we shall see his face no
more. And we are glad and thankful that his memory shall
dwell here as a benediction in days to come.

REMINISCENCES OF JOSEPH LE CONTE.

BY JOHN MUIR.

"BEYOND all wealth, honor, or even health, is the attach-
ment we form to noble souls."

I have been one of Joseph Le Conte's innumerable friends
and admirers for more than thirty years. It was in Yosemite
Valley that I first met him, not far from the famous rock be-
neath the shadow of which he died. With a party of his
students he was making his first excursion into the high
Sierra, and it was delightful to see with what eager, joyful,
youthful enthusiasm he reveled in the sublime beauty of the
great Valley, and tried to learn how it was made. His fame
had already reached me, though he had then been only a year
or two in California, and, like everybody else, I was at once
drawn to him by the charm of his manners, as to a fine lake
or a mountain; and when he kindly invited me to join his
party, of course I gladly left all my other work and followed
him. This first Le Conte excursion, with its grand landscapes
and weather and delightful campfire talks, though now far
back in the days of auld lang syne, still remains in mind
bright and indestructible, like glacial inscriptions on granite.

We left the Valley by the Coulterville trail, then, turning to the eastward, climbed in long, wavering curves and zigzags through the glorious forests of silver fir north of Yosemite, across the dome-paved basin of Yosemite Creek, along the southern slopes of Mt. Hoffmann, down into the bright, icy basin of Lake Tenaya, over the Merced and Tuolumne divide past a multitude of sublime glacial monuments, along many a mile of smooth, flowery meadows, up Mt. Dana, and down Bloody Cañon to the lake and gray plains and volcanoes of Mono. How the beloved Professor enjoyed all this his own story best tells. Sinewy, slender, erect, he studied the grand show, forgetting all else, riding with loose, dangling rein, allowing his horse to go as it liked. He had a fine poetic appreciation of nature, and never tired of gazing at the noble forests and gardens, lakes and meadows, mountains and streams, displayed along the windings of the trail, calling attention to this and that with buoyant, sparkling delight like that of a child, keeping up running all-day lectures, as if trying to be the tongue of every object in sight. On calm nights by the campfire he talked on the lessons of the day, blending art, science, and philosophy with whatever we had seen. Any one of us, by asking a question on no matter what subject, made his thoughts pour forth and shine like rain, quickening, exciting mental action, appealing to all that is noblest in life.

Our camp at Lake Tenaya was especially memorable. After supper and some talk by the fire, Le Conte and I sauntered through the pine groves to the shore and sat down on a big rock that stands out a little way in the water. The full moon and the stars filled the lake with light, and brought out the rich sculpture of the walls of the basin and surrounding mountains with marvelous clearness and beauty amid the shadows. Subsiding waves made gentle heaving swells, and a slight breeze ruffled the surface, giving rise to ever-changing pictures of wondrous brightness. At first we talked freely, admiring the silvery masses and ripples of light, and the mystic, wavering dance of the stars and rocks and shadows re-

flected in the unstable mirror. But soon came perfect still-
ness, earth and sky were inseparably blended and spiritual-
ized, and we could only gaze on the celestial vision in devout,
silent, wondering admiration. That lake with its mountains
and stars, pure, serene, transparent, its boundaries lost in
fullness of light, is to me an emblem of the soul of our
friend.

Two years later we again camped together, when I was
leading him to some small residual glaciers I had found. But
his time was short; he had to get back to his class-room. I
suggested running away for a season or two in time-obliterat-
ing wildness, and pictured the blessings that would flow from
truancy so pious and glorious. He smiled in sympathy with
an introverted look, as if recalling his own free days when
first he reveled in nature's wild wealth. I think it was at
this time he told me the grand story of his early exploring
trip to Lake Superior and the then wild region about the
headwaters of the Mississippi. And notwithstanding he accomplished so much in the short excursions which at every
opportunity he made, I have always thought it was to be re-
gretted that he allowed himself to be caught and put in pro-
fessional harness so early.

As a teacher he stood alone on this side of the
continent, and his influence no man can measure. He
carried his students in his heart, and was the idol of the
University. He had the genius of hard work which not
even the lassitude of sickness could stop. Few of his scholars
knew with what inexorable determination he toiled to keep
close up with the most advanced thought of the times and get
it into teachable form; how he listened to the speech which
day uttereth unto day, and gathered knowledge from every
source—libraries, laboratories, explorers in every field, assim-
ilating the results of other men's discoveries and making them
his own, to be given out again free as air. He had the rare
gift of making dim, nebulous things clear and attractive to
other minds, and he never lacked listeners. Always ready for

every sort of audience, he lifted his charmed hearers up and away into intellectual regions they had never hoped to see or dared to encounter, making the ways seem easy, paths of pleasantness and peace, like a mountaineer who, anxious to get others onto commanding peaks, builds a trail for them, winding hither and thither through the midst of toil-beguiling beauty to summits whence the infinitely varied features of the landscape are seen in one harmony, and all boundaries are transparent and become outlets into celestial space.

Joseph Le Conte was not a leader, and he was as far as possible from being what is called "a good fighter, or hater." Anything like a quarrel or hot controversy he instinctively avoided, went serenely on his way, steeping everything in philosophy, overcoming evil with good. His friends were all who knew him, and he had besides the respect of the whole community, hopefully showing that however bad the world may be, it is good enough to recognize a good man.

In the winter of 1874 or '5 I made the acquaintance of his beloved brother, John. The two with their families were then living together in a queer old house in Oakland, and I spent many pleasant evenings with them. The brothers and John's son Julian were invariably found reading or writing. Joseph, turning down his book, would draw me out on my studies in the Sierra, and we were occasionally joined by John when some interesting question of physics caught his attention,—the carrying force of water at different velocities, how boulders were shoved or rolled on sea beaches or in river channels, glacial denudation, etc. I noticed that when difficulties on these and kindred subjects came up Joseph turned to his brother, and always, I think, regarded him intellectually as greater than himself. Once he said to me: "The public don't know my brother for half what he is; only in purely scientific circles is he known. There he is well known and appreciated as one of the greatest physicists in America. He seems to have less vitality than I have, seldom lectures outside of his classroom, cares nothing for popularity; but he is one of the most

amiable of men as well as one of the most profound and original of thinkers." In face and manners he was like his
brother, and had the same genial disposition and intellectual
power. But he was less influential as a teacher than Joseph,
held straighter forward on his own way, doing original and
purely scientific work, and loved to dwell on the heights out
of sight of common minds. Few of his students could follow
him in his lectures, for his aims were high and the trails he
made were steep, but all were his devoted admirers. Until
John's death, some ten years ago, the brothers were always
spoken of as "the two Le Contes." In my mind they still
stand together, a blessed pair, twin stars of purest light.
Their writings brought them world-wide renown, and their
names will live, but far more important is the inspiring, up-
lifting, enlightening influence they exerted on their students
and the community, which, spreading from mind to mind,
heart to heart, age to age, in ever widening circles, will go on
forever.

JOSEPH LE CONTE.

BY INA COOLBRITH.

What words can add unto his fame,
 Or greener make his well-won bays?
Himself has deathless writ his name.
 His life-work is his noblest praise.

No man was cast in gentler mould,
 Yet stronger none in firm command.
His thought our lesser thought controlled,
 Our hearts he held within his hand.

And Heaven so close about him lay
 While still earth's lowly plane he trod,
He might not miss its shining way:
 Who walks with nature walks with God.

THE GEOLOGICAL WORK OF PROFESSOR JOSEPH LE CONTE.

BY JOHN C. MERRIAM.

PROFESSOR LE CONTE seems to have been first attracted to geological work by coming in contact with Dr. James Hall, the famous leader of the earlier geological school in this country. Up to the time of his first meeting with Hall, he had shown interest in geology, but was principally concerned with problems belonging in other branches of science. Though the first great stimulus to this work was received from Hall, his career in this field really began after his interests became identified with those of the University of California. The greater number of his contributions to geological science, both descriptive and philosophic, are based upon observations made on the Pacific Coast.

Professor Le Conte's work was in general the study of the greater problems in geology, rather than the description of isolated phenomena. He never mistook the geological symbol for the thing it represented, and he was never mislead by anything foreign to the problem he sought to solve.

Though not generally considered a field geologist, he made extensive excursions to the regions of greatest interest on this coast. A considerable part of the Sierra range was explored by him, and his mountain study was carried north into Oregon and Washington. On his summer excursions he was not infrequently accompanied by students from his classes in the University.

Although his greatest interest seems to have centered around problems concerning the relation of the greater physical changes, especially crustal movements, to the evolution of the organic world, he furnished important contributions to nearly all branches of geology. On the purely mineralogical or chemical side, we find him adding to our knowledge of metalliferous veins, and he is generally recognized as one of the authorities on this subject. On the physical side, he interested himself in the carrying power of water and in the exact study of earthquake waves. In palæontological work his description and discussion of the famous Carson footprints, which was actually the first on that subject to be completed, is a truly remarkable piece of investigation. Much of his most important work was in the field of general inorganic geology. Here he contributed largely to the literature on the origin and formation of mountains, the evolution of continental masses, the permanence of continents and ocean basins, movements of the earth's crust and their causes, the great lava flood of the northwest, Mono volcanoes, and the glacial geology of the Sierras. He was also an active worker in historical geology, and some of his latest publications on critical periods in the earth's history and the Sierran (Ozarkian) epoch open practically new territory for research.

The work which Professor Le Conte accomplished in geology shows throughout a conception of the relations of the various branches of natural science to each other such as has been possessed by but few. To the close of his life he kept himself perfectly informed on all the important work being done in the natural history sciences, and owing to his wide field of vision he was frequently able to determine at a glance the proper relation of things, which others, limited to a narrow field, could not possibly discern. This is shown very frequently in his combination of the good points of several quite different theories bearing on the same subject. Many of his contributions, more especially those on critical periods in the earth's history, show just such a grasp of the whole subject of geological and biological science. In this work he called attention, as had never been done before, to the effect of complex physical changes, such as critical movements and modifications of climate on the progress of organic evolution.

Through all of his contributions to historical geology, there runs as the central idea the theory of organic evolution. The fossil forms preserved to us from past periods were not considered by him simply as curiosities which were interesting because they happened to appear strange to us, but rather as the sacred remains left by a countless succession of generations which has passed to us, along an unbroken chain, the principle or germ of life. Probably no other writer in the field ef historical geology has made such successful use of the evolutionary or narrative style of the treatment of the subject. Though Professor Le Conte ascribes the first use of this method to Dana, it is probably true that his own work had great influence in finally bringing Dana to the point where he could unreservedly accept evolution as based on actual historic succession. In his later lectures and discussions of the theory of evolution, to which he has contributed so much, he placed the strongest emphasis on what *has been* rather than what *might be.*

In his intercourse with other scientific men Professor Le Conte was always helpful, sympathetic, and appreciative. He always gave freely of his store of knowledge in assisting others to solve problems which refused to yield to them. Though he engaged in many discussions with those whose views differed from his own, he made no enemies. Always respecting others' opinions, whether he accepted them or not, he was ever held in the highest respect and esteem by geologists of all lands. In recognition of his services to geological science, Professor Le Conte was honored by election to the highest positions which the scientific associations of this country could confer. He served as President of the American Geological Society and of the American Association for the Advancement of Science, and had been Vice-President of the International Geological Congress.

As far-reaching and as lasting as Professor Le Conte's influence may be seen to be among the men of his profession, it will probably not exceed that which he has exerted on the world at large in the capacity of instructor. In his own classroom at the University of California during more than thirty years, he presented to interested audiences the best that there is in his subject. Such was his power of explanation and description in the lecture room that the most difficult problems seemed absolutely to melt away, and after hearing him on such subjects students have been known to state that explanation seemed hardly necessary, as the matter was so easily understood. Through the medium of his text-book, "The Elements of Geology," he has covered a vastly larger field than could be reached in his lectures. Probably no college text-book in science has been more widely used in this country than "The Elements." Certainly, there are none which present in a simpler or more attractive form the elements of any science. His treatment of the subject was, when his book first appeared, in many respects essentially new, and almost for the first time it was made clear that geological history is only the earlier part of history in general.

With the passing of Professor Le Conte, geologists lose a great contributor and leader, and the world loses a great teacher. Others may arise who in scientific attainment in this particular branch of research will perhaps stand in the same rank with him, but it will be long before we find again in one man that combination of qualities which has made Professor Le Conte not only one of the most successful gatherers of knowledge, but also one of the foremost teachers.

PROFESSOR LE CONTE AS SEEN THROUGH HIS BIOLOGICAL WORK.

BY WM. E. RITTER.

IT is not my purpose to give here either a historical review of Professor Joseph Le Conte's biological work or a critical estimate of its value. The former would not be of much interest in itself. The latter, if done at all by any of us who were his intimate associates, must be a task for the future after time shall have given his deeds chance to regain in our minds some portion of the room now filled by the sense of deprivation and grief at the departure from us forever of the rare man, the beloved master, the dear friend. What interests us now above all else is the man himself.

My primary aim shall be consequently to make the consideration of his biological work contribute to the gaining of a fuller and clearer view of the man, his life, his ideals.

Professor Le Conte's first allegiance was to geology rather than biology. He himself freely owned this, and it was universally recognized among his scientific contemporaries. It is significant, however, that his early training was more biological than geological; that some of his earliest and his very last scientific papers were biological; and that his most original and probably most enduring work was in this domain.

The study and practice of medicine, to which he devoted seven years, between the ages of twenty and twenty-seven, were for him, as they should be for all devotees of this noble profession, a biological matter; and later his training under Louis Agassiz was more biological than geological, for Agassiz was primarily a zoologist.

Among his earliest writings, the papers which bring out best not only the scope but also the philosophical cast of his knowledge in the biological sciences, three are preëminent.

The first, chronologically, published in 1850 while he was still a practicing physician, is "On the Science of Medicine, and Causes Which Have Retarded Its Progress." The second, bearing the date of 1858 and entitled "Morphology and Its Connection With Fine Art," gives more fully and clearly than can be gained elsewhere the doctrine of organic creation then held by him. The third, read at the American Association for the Advancement of Science in 1859 and published the same year, is on "The Correlation of Physical, Chemical and Vital Force, and the Conservation of Force in Vital Phenomena." This is undoubtedly one of his most important contributions to biological thought. His very last published words are in the form of a note in *Science*, June 21, 1901, on "What Is Life?" His investigations in sight, particularly in binocular vision, were, in his own estimation, the most original and independent of his work.

I believe, too, that in his biological rather than his geological writings we find most fully displayed the catholicity of his mind toward natural phenomena. Nowhere in geology did he penetrate deeply in technical minutiæ. Had we his geological work only to judge from, we might conclude that he was deficient in the capacity for and delight in that patient, minute working out of details so essential to the highest, safest achievement in any province of physical science. One has, however, but to follow through carefully Part III of the last edition of the volume on "Sight" to find that he did possess it in an eminent degree. Here, far more than anywhere else in his published writings, is displayed the mathematical-physical quality of his mind, which he inherited from his father, and which came out so prominently in his brother, John Le Conte.

His way of seeing natural phenomena in the large, and his remarkable power of finding the unifying principles and laws underlying them, though perhaps brought to bear in geology more fruitfully for the science itself than in biology, is shown in its full breadth, and to the understanding of a larger public

in biology than in geology.   His numerous discussions of the
relation of science to education, art, sociology, philosophy, and
religion, have undoubtedly had the widest influence of all his
works on the thought of his generation.

A systematic examination of his utterances in this province
shows them to be essentially a defence of the proposition that
human life, whatever else it may be, is still fundamentally
akin to all life; and hence that the basal idea of biology—
Life; and the distinctive method of biological science, the
comparative method—must be carried into all investigation and
treatment of human life and society.

Nearly all his papers of this class are, in keeping with
this general purpose, first, a presentation of the data and
fundamental conceptions of biology with some illustration of
the comparative method; and, second, a projection of these
data and conceptions and methods into the particular topic
under consideration.

For example, his early essay on "Morphology and Its
Connection With Fine Art," already referred to, is quite an
extensive treatise on the doctrine of organic types held at that
time by some of the foremost biologists, with a consideration
of the laws of modification within the types.   These types are
the expression of Divine *ideas;* the working out of them in
nature is God's way of giving his ideas *form*.   Nature, then,
is Divine art wrought out by the hand of the Divine artist.
Human art is true art, consequently, in so far as it obeys the
laws and follows the example of Divine art, which is nature.

This early paper illustrates so well the method of all his
later thinking in these directions, it will be profitable to see
some of its expressions themselves.   "We have seen," he
says, "that in all organic nature we find everywhere some
simple idea infinitely modified.   Differentiation of a simple
elementary form and specialization of function, resulting in
mutual dependence of parts, is the fundamental idea of organization, the very idea of life, the very principle of *Divine
architecture*.   Now, is not this the principle, too, unconsciously

applied, of the highest human architecture? In the best spec-
imens of Gothic architecture—*e. g.*, how often do we find the
same elementary form repeated *ad infiniteum*, under various
disguises, according to the functions of the several parts.
* * * Is not this differentiation of simple elementary form
and specialization of function? Is it not the mutual and har-
monious dependence of parts which constitutes true organic
unity? Is it not organization? Is it not life? We believe
that this idea of organic unity is the basis of all art.''

Likewise, an analysis of his numerous papers on the relation of biology to sociology will show the same thing: A
setting forth of the data and conceptions and methods of biological science first; then the application of these to the science of human society.

I must not dwell further on this matter. It will suffice
for the present to point out that of the 340 pages constituting
the volume on ''Evolution and Its Relation to Religious
Thought,'' 250 are a treatise on organic evolution, pure and
simple.

The preponderance of his early training distinctly on the
side of biology; possessed of so strong a predilection for philosophical contemplation of the phenomena of life, and such
sympathy for it as it manifests itself in human kind, the question inevitably arises, why did he choose to make geology
rather than biology his central concern?

It should be observed that the decision could not have rested
in this instance as in many another on the ground of the mere
circumstance of a position for winning a livelihood; for each
of the college professorships he was called to fill at various
times during his life included, like that in our own University, the two sciences on an equal footing.

He has told us that it was his meeting with James Hall,
for many years Chief of the New York State Geological Sur-
vey, that was the immediate influence in turning him to
geology. But there must have been something deeper than
mere contact with a man; deeper than any exterior influence,

in it.   He did not meet Hall, if I remember correctly, until some time after he had become a regular student under Agassiz; and it can hardly be supposed that Hall's enthusiasm, great as it is said to have been, could have been in itself a greater winning force than Agassiz's.

Strongly as biological phenomena appealed to his mind, he must have found something in geology that attracted him still more.   Without presuming to have recognized positively and fully what that something was, I believe we can detect at least a part of it.

I think we may say that the science of organisms did indeed appeal to him more than any other; but for him the earth was an organism.   It had a beginning in a simple, homogeneous state; it has undergone a continuous, orderly development in time through the operation of its resident forces; it will have an end.

The contemplation of *forces* and *processes* was to him the thing of supreme interest everywhere.   In the biological province, it was not the structure of the eye, but its mode of working and its evolution that engaged his attention.   It was not the histology of the liver, but its glycogenic function that interested him; not wing anatomy, but the flight of birds was it that he found delight in studying.

So in geology it was not the structure of mountains, but the way they were built; not the composition of ore deposits, but the method of their formation that he thought upon with such zeal and pleasure and acumen.

Now, the earth being for him an organism, because it is the mightiest of all organisms, it attracted him more than any other.

His mind could not be satisfied with generalizations about nature until they had reached out to its uttermost limits, and in the infinite time of geology and the immensity of earth-developing forces, he found room for the unhampered play of his scientific imagination and unexcelled powers of generalization, that he did not find in biology.

One other insight into his nature, properly obtained by approaching him from the biological direction, I must touch upon in conclusion. I refer to his attitude toward the doctrine of evolution. This admirably illustrates both his absolute fealty to scientific truth and the depth and sincerity of his devotion to the essentials of religion.

The particularly admirable and significant thing about this attitude is not that he stood as one of the ablest, fairest-minded champions of both religion and evolution, but the fact of his having become such a champion. It is a less distinction for him that he *did* write the "Evolution in Its Relation to Religious Thought" than that he *could* write it. Weighty as are the arguments on the printed pages of the book for the fundamental accord of scientific and religious truth, weightier still, I think, are those it contains that are not printed at all. It is the life of the man; the history of the development of his mind, to be read only between the lInes, that should give it its greatest value, particularly for those of its readers who stand chiefly on the side of religion.

Professor Le Conte did not become an evolutionist fully until he was fifty years old, and for most of his life before this he was very far from being one. Listen to this and see what a strange sound it has in contrast with what we have all been so accustomed to hear him teach: "They [organic species] have remained unchanged in spite of changes in physical conditions. * * * Physical conditions *may destroy but not transmute them.* * * * The conclusion, therefore, is irresistible, that organic forms have no physical cause, but they must be referred directly to the Great First Cause, or else that each species has a distinct immaterial essence, which is the cause of its specific form." These sentences were being written in 1858, the very year in which Darwin's great discovery of natural selection was first given to the world. The conceptions nevertheless here given expression to were held by him essentially for another decade at least; until the "Origin of Species" had been long before the world, and after most biologists had gone over to the evolutionary side. Now, a superficial consideration of the matter might regard his slowness in accepting the doctrine as savoring somewhat of narrowness and bigotry. But two facts that stand out clear enough as soon as we look more carefully must dispel even a suggestion of such an interpretation. In the first place, so much to him by both nature and nurture was his *religious faith*—not his *theological creed*—that it would have been self-destructive for him to accept any scientific doctrine that his reason affirmed to be in deadly opposition to that faith. To estimate him fairly here, one must consider carefully his religious nature and training. Into this it is not my province to enter now.

In the second place, it must be understood that in all things and always he was philosophical. A common meeting ground he always must have for two elements so large and precious to his life as were his science and his religion. This he found for biological science in the doctrine of organic types, first made prominent in zoology by Cuvier, and later adopted and defended by Sir Richard Owen and Louis Agassiz, three of the greatest names, perhaps, it must be observed, in the whole history of the sciences of comparative anatomy and palæontology.

Four and only four great types of animal organization, this doctrine said. Four and only four Divine conceptions or plans in the whole animal creation, round which all the myriad variety of forms have been wrought out by modification through the infinite wisdom and power and resource of the Divine Architect. All the kinds of living things are the thoughts of God.

No conception of organic creation has ever been proposed that appeals to the poetic imagination so strongly as this; none more better adapted to a naïve faith in a personal Deity imminent in the natural world.

It is certainly a lofty, ennobling conception, one that has satisfied, in one form and another, both the religious and the scientific needs of some of the greatest biologists that have lived. Cuvier, Owen, Agassiz, and Le Conte held it, and it is worth while to be reminded that the last three were contemporaries for much of their lives and that all of them were born a number of years before Cuvier died. Of them all, Le Conte was the only one who gave up the doctrine and became an evolutionist.

For a man of such nature as Joseph Le Conte's to have wholly reconstructed his religious faith and philosophy on a higher plane after forty-five, is certainly one of the hardest, noblest acts he could possibly perform.

PROFESSOR LE CONTE AS A PHILOSOPHER.

BY CHARLES M. BAKEWELL.

STUDENTS of philosophy have especial occasion to mourn the loss of Professor Le Conte. He was one of the last representatives of that nobler race of scientists who labored incessantly to find through their very scientific investigations a larger and richer world-view; who sought through science a way of life more religious than that of the ordinary traditional believer, more philosophic than that of the ordinary cloistral philosopher. Scientists of the present generation are apt to be more timid, to have an unwholesome dread of the charge of being "unscientific," and to hesitate, at least in print, to step beyond the prescribed limits of their chosen fields of investigation.

Professor Le Conte was, to be sure, interested in his science for its own sake, and attained marked eminence among his specialist brethren; but he was, first of all, a man, interested in all things human, and particularly in those questions that go deepest into human nature, which are precisely the questions of philosophy and religion. He knew that, as a man, he did not live merely in the world of geology, or in the world of biology; that, as a man, he was bound to take sides implying a definite attitude toward all reality. He knew that one's "way of life" is in itself an implicit philosphy, true or false; and, believing thus philosophy to be inevitable, he held, with Socrates, that "an unexamined life is not worthy to be lived by a *man*."

The master generalization of science of his day is contained in the the theory of evolution,—a theory which certainly at first sight seems to make of man a mere thing among things, a mere creature of cosmic causes, and therefore neither free, nor yet immortal; a theory which seems to substitute for the personal God of religion a blind, immanent force. Professor Le Conte was but gradually won over to full acceptance of this theory, of which he was to become such a famous expounder, and this fact was due, I think, to religious misgivings quite as much as to scientific caution. "Our faith in the Infinite Righteousness," he used to say, "is founded on just the same ground as our indestructible faith in the Reign of Law in the natural world, and is just as reasonable."* And so he must first assure himself that the theory of evolution did no violence to the moral needs of man, for he felt that if it did, it must in the end do violence to his intellectual needs as well.

However that may be, Professor Le Conte's contributions to philosophy are found in his discussions of these cardinal questions: the existence of God, the freedom and immortality of man, and the closely allied question as to the meaning of evil.

From one point of view his work here seems mainly to consist in the attempt to quash the negative answer, which some over-confident evolutionists would forthworth make to these questions, and to do this by emphasizing the fact that the theory of evolution, being simply a reading of the *way* in which phenomena occur, can tell us nothing with regard to the *ground* of phenomena, and therefore as lit-

---

*"The Conception of God," p. 71.

tle affects our idealism, our theism, or our views with regard
to the moral problem, as does any other generalization of science, for example, the law of gravitation. All such generalizations, to be sure, unify experience, and in so far eliminate
the possibility of special providence. The evolutionist must
therefore indeed say: If there is a God, he is in very much
more intimate relation to nature and to man than is supposed
in popular anthropomorphic conceptions of deity; if there is a
free and immortal soul, none the less, the body, with which
the soul is in some mysterious way united, must appear simply as one particular physical fact, having its place in a world
of such facts completely unified by the conception of evolution.

There is, however, Professor Le Conte held, an inner as
well as an outer aspect of experience; there are feelings,
thoughts, volitions, as well as stocks and stones, matter and
motion. No one has ever succeeded, or, he added, ever will
succeed, in showing how the material evolves into the mental,
how motion in matter—even nervous matter—can be trans-
muted into thought. There is an impassable gulf fixed between these two orders of experience.* Has, then, evolution
nothing to say with regard to this inner aspect of experience?
Yes. When psychology becomes comparative psychology we
are able to trace a separate evolutional process in the mental
series that is precisely analogous to the evolutional process in
the physical series. Thus we are led to believe that "the
spirit of man was developed out of the *anima* or conscious
principle of animals, and that this, again, was developed out
of the lower forms of life-force, and this in its turn out of the
chemical and physical forces of Nature, and that at a certain
stage in this gradual development, viz., with man, it *acquired*
the property of immortality."† And Professor Le Conte was
fond of picturing, in characteristically striking imagery, the
manner in which the evolutional process may be conceived as

*"Evolution and Its Relation to Religious Thought," pp. 290 ff.
†Op. cit., p, 205.

preparing the way for the final emergence of the free and im.
mortal spirit.*

If we carry the analogy of the relation between inner and
outer over to the entire world of nature, then God may be
conceived as the *anima mundi*, and the world of things, while
remaining mere objects *for us*, as stubborn and refractory as
you please, may be conceived as God's thoughts objectified,—†
a position that suggests Berkeley's famous saying that nature is "Divine visual language," is God's way of talking to
man.   God is regarded, in other words, as immanent in nature; the physical and chemical forces are a part of the Divine
energy "in a diffused, unindividuated state."   Gradually a
part of this part becomes individuated and self-active, at first
partially so, in plant and animal, at last completely so, in man
as a moral person.‡

Professor Le Conte did not, however, rest content with
showing how the world might be conceived from the stand-
point of evolution so as not to interfere with our fundamental
religious beliefs, and thus leave the door open for faith to
bring them in.   He held that the theory of evolution furnished a positive inductive argument for the existence of
God, and for the immortality of the soul.   Evolution discov-
ers a general trend of development, an upward and onward
progress, which clearly points beyond to the perfect goal.
The meaning of the whole process, and of every part of it, is
found in this perfect goal, which must therefore be as real as
any of the steps to which it gives meaning.

Similarly in the case of the individual, the meaning of the
struggle from consciousness to self-consciousness, and of the
further struggles in the journey through life from consciousness to moral consciousness, is lost if death end all, for then
man must be forever chasing an *ignis fatuus*, forever stretch-

---

*Esp. op. cit., p. 300.   The metaphors here used frequently recur in Professor Le
Conte's writings.

†Op. cit., p. 283.

‡"Conceptions of God," p. 76.

ing out after ideals hopelessly beyond his reach. Further-
more, the sole purpose of the progressive individuation of the
Divine energy by evolution is that God may have in man
"something not only to contemplate, but also to love and be
loved by." And "without immortality this whole purpose is
balked—the whole process of cosmic evolution is futile."*

The position is thus, at bottom, a simple expression of trust
in the complete rationality of the universe, a profession of
faith in reason which has become a faith but the more surely
grounded by the scientific discoveries of the orderliness and
reasonableness of nature's ways.

In his treatment of the problem of evil Professor Le Conte
held that physical evil is the necessary price of the intelligent,
moral evil the inevitable condition of the moral, personality.
Men might conceivably have been created innocent, but not
morally good. Choice of the good, which morality implies, is
only possible for one who has also the knowledge of evil.
And the sting which lurks in this doctrine, so far as moral
degenerates and other unfortunates are concerned, is removed by the conviction of the essential deathlessness of the
self-conscious personality.

Professor Le Conte's favorite method consisted in bringing
forward upon each topic treated two opposing, and apparently
equally plausible, views, and then showing that usually each
was right in what it asserted and wrong in what it denied;
that both were partial truths which could be welded together
into a higher synthesis,—a method which to the student of
philosophy will at once suggest the Hegelian dialectic, with
its triune forward movement.

Suggestive also of Hegel is Professor Le Conte's general
conception of reality as one eternal consciousness which
"outers" itself in the world of nature, while remaining one
with itself throughout, is immanent in this world as its one
moving principle; and his method of escape from the panthe-
ism implied in this view by holding that this consciousness is

---

*"The Conception of God," pp. 77-8.

Infinite Benevolence, and that it is the very life of its being to bring to life other beings, which, while springing from it, shall be none the less independent and free, the responsible agents of their own deeds.

If asked to explain *how* this could be, and further, *how* a free spirit could originate acts in a world ruled by divine law and necessity,—as he held the world to be,—Professor Le Conte would shake his head and reply in his well-known, deliberate, emphatic way: "I do not know. It is a *mystery*, but a mystery upon which we may not unreasonably hope some day to have more light."

In what I have said above I have confined myself strictly to a statement of Professor Le Conte's position, made, as far as possible, in his own words. Brief as the statement is, it will, I trust, make evident the fact that Professor Le Conte's was a genuinely philosophical mind. We can only regret that he did not find occasion, amid the stress of other duties, to elaborate and develop more in detail his philosophical views, and particularly his significant attempt to effect the "higher synthesis" of monism and pluralism by regarding reality as originally One, but, at the same time, as a One whose very life-purpose it is to acheive, through means of nature, a world of many spirits, each of whom is independent and fiee and absolutely real, and, therefore, capable of communing with Him,—a view which he summed up in the sentence; "Nature is the womb *in* which, and evolution the process *by* which, are generated sons of God."*

This is a unique position which must henceforth be reckoued with by all who would comprehend this all-important philosophical issue.

*"The Conception of God," p. 78.

JOSEPH LE CONTE AT YOSEMITE.
JULY 4-6, 1901.

BY EDWARD ROBESON TAYLOR.

"If it were now to die,
'T were now to be most happy "
Othello

His hoary head, lustrous with all that's best
   Of humankind, by fame immortal made,
   In death's last agony he meetly laid
Upon Yosemite's titanic breast.
For years their mutual love had been confessed,
   And when once more her glories he surveyed,
   Such raptures in his deepest bosom played,
Fate dared not tempt him further to be blest.
Her beauteous leaves of cedar, oak and pine,
   She lavish gave for garlands to entwine
   His coffin fashioned from her teeming store ;
And 'neath the reverent gaze of her great walls,
   While throbbed in muffled tones her saddened falls
   His clay, star-lighted, left her evermore.

AN ESTIMATE OF THE LIFE WORK OF DR. JOSEPH LE CONTE.

BY EUGENE W. HILGARD.

THE death of Dr. Joseph Le Conte removes one of the foremost thinkers and scientific men of the time; one whose writings and modes of thought have influenced the progress of science, and of scientific as well as popular opinion, throughout the civilized world. He was prominent in the now fast-thinning ranks of those who, like Louis Agassiz, J. D. Dana and Asa Gray, in the New, and Lyell, Oersted, Darwin and Wallace, in the Old World, thought and found it not only possible but necessary to be something more than specialists in one domain of science, in order to understand its full meanings and bearings upon other branches, and its place in the world-plan. Le Conte never doubted the existence of such a plan, and he looked upon nature reverently as one part of its manifestations; but without undervaluing for a moment the other, the spiritual part, which is now so commonly cast aside as a mere "property of matter in an advanced state of evolution;" while, on the other hand, there are still those who claim to evolve its nature from their inner consciousness, independently of observed phenomena. Le Conte's early education and experience as a physician laid the foundations of the broad knowledge which later made him equally at home in the purely physical sciences and in the biological field. While his geological writings are, perhaps, best known to the American public, through the wide use made of his books on that subject, both in universities and in the secondary schools, his early and warm advocacy of the doctrine of evolution has probably served most to make him known and appreciated in the Old World, where he was warmly welcomed and honored in scientific assemblies, among the foremost men. His election to the Presidency of the International Geological Congress, held at Washington in 1891, and to that of the American Association for the Advancement of Science in 1892, were manifestations of the high esteem in which he was held by his scientific colleagues.

It is sometimes said that those who undertake to generalize in science are apt to be unable to make accurate observations themselves. While this is true in some cases, it was certainly otherwise in that of Le Conte. His scientific writings and special papers show an eminent capacity for close observation; yet his glance was always upon the bearings of what he saw, upon general problems rather than upon the minor details of each field of view, which he was quite content to leave to others. At the same time, he had the true scientific spirit in the absence of all dogmatism, and the readiness at all times to consider candidly any observations or opinions at variance with his previous conclusions. He considered the cultivation of the spirit of truthfulness, candor, and readiness to revise one's opinions and conclusions, as constituting one of the strongest claims of natural science as an educational factor; in contradistinction to the acceptance of mere opinions and precedents that is so common a result of exclusive literary and philosophical study. The personal gentleness for which he was so well known and beloved, was deeply grounded in the absence of any claim to infallibility for himself.

It is not easy to overestimate the influence he has exerted in rectifying the popular idea that the doctrine of evolution necessarily tends to materialism, if not atheism; a misconception of its true import which is unfortunately still shared in by the extremists both on the scientific and religious side. Le Conte held that so far from this, it inculcates the highest ideal of an intelligent world-plan; and he staunchly maintained not only its compatibility with Christian religious belief, but that by elevating nature into the realm of teleologic thought and aspiration, it offers a much higher point of view than could be derived from any of the "orthodox" views of the method of Creation. This part of his influence will, perhaps, be most missed in the present state and tendency of scientific thought; particularly among the younger men of science, whose eagerness to specialize prematurely almost inevitably tends to prevent such catholicity of views and encyclopedic knowledge as characterized Dr. Le Conte. Among the means by which he was enabled to maintain a working acquaintance with the rapid progress in all the sciences, was his habit of conscientiously keeping up a compact but comprehensive *"index rerum,"* in which he noted all the new or otherwise important scientific and philosophic papers that came under his notice; and his ready reference to the latest investigations and discussions of almost any of the subjects in which he was interested—and there were few in which he was not—was a constant surprise to those who consulted him. He thus avoided overloading his mind with a multitude of details not necessary to the main questions involved. It is hoped that this precious record will be deposited in the library of the University.

It was Le Conte through whom the University of California first became known to the outside world as a school and center of science on the western border of the continent; and for a number of years he almost alone kept it in view of the world of science. His presence and connection with the University was largely instrumental in attracting to it other men who otherwise would have hesitated to emigrate from their Eastern homes to what was then the outskirts of civilization; and his ceaseless scientific activity acted as a strong stimulus both to his colleagues and to the students coming under his instruction, whose affection and esteem remained with him through life. He preferred this kind of activity to the more ambitious prospects that were many times open to him; he shrank from anything that would force him from the ideal world in which he lived, into active contact with executive or administrative functions. His modesty and simplicity survived, unscathed, the applause and laudations bestowed upon him, and his strong will and cheerful disposition carried him up to a mature age in undiminished mental vigor, despite an apparently frail body.

His death brings heavy loss to the University and to the world of thought at large. His place cannot be filled, and the statement that no attempt will be made to do so, is but a natural expression of the high and exceptional position he occupied in the world of science.

THE UNPUBLISHED WORKS OF JOSEPH LE CONTE.

BY MARY BELL.

AT the time of Professor Le Conte's death in the Yosemite Valley, on July 6, 1901, he had completed the autobiography of his life. This work, consisting of probably two hundred thousand words, was written in Georgia during the winter before his death. Professor Le Conte also left a journal of three months' personal experiences during the last days of the Confederacy. This is full of exciting details of the rescue of his daughter from the Federal lines and the burning of Columbia. Besides these are innumerable unpublished lectures, after-dinner speeches and many pamphlets that have not yet been collected in a permanent form.

In the autobiography of Joseph Le Conte, there is a long account of his Huguenot ancestry. Guillaume Le Conte fled from Rouen after the revocation of the edict of Nantes, served under William of Orange in England and finally came to America in 1698, settling near New York. Louis Le Conte, ten years after graduating from Columbia in 1800, removed to Liberty County, Georgia, where he had inherited a large plantation. Here he married Ann Quarterman, a lady of English Puritan descent, and of these parents Joseph Le Conte was born February 26, 1823. There were seven children, Joseph being the youngest of the four sons.

The best of Joseph Le Conte's early education was received on the large plantation where every kind of industry was conducted, including weaving, spinning, shoemaking, the manufacturing of farm implements and harness and the making of firearms. All of the necessaries, even some of the luxuries of life on the old Southern plantation, were produced where the Le Conte children could daily watch the negro laborers at work under the overseers. The boys frequently entered with interest into the work of farming and manufacturing. There is a long account, in the autobiography, of the making of a gun by one of the older brothers in the family.

Like all Southern boys the Le Contes were taught the use of a gun, and Joseph was congratulated upon the killing of his first squirrel at a very early age. The death of the little animal, however, caused the young hunter more grief than pride in his achievement.

The father of Joseph Le Conte was a man of great culture, possessed of a fine scientific mind. His relation to his children was intimate and very beautiful, and he took great pains to give them opportunities for observation and the accumulation of practical knowledge. Long before the days of kindergartens, he instinctively trained his children by the best of those methods. His mother was very musical and artistic, and from her Joseph received the taste for the beautiful that ennobled his science.

The Le Conte children daily walked to the little country school, followed by a small negro with their lunch basket. Of the teachers in this school none influenced the life of Joseph to any extent, save Alexander Stephens, afterwards vice-president of the Confederacy and governor of his state. Georgia conferred upon Stephens every possible honor. Professor Le Conte frequently met Mr. Stephens in the South and in Washington, and the famous statesman always spoke of the great influence that Louis Le Conte had exerted over him.

When Joseph entered the University of Georgia, he was strong, athletic, a good swimmer, fond of the hunt and of all out of door life. In the University his place was recognized as that of a distinguished student, an athlete and a debator. In the Phi Kappa Society, he took part in many debates, thereby gaining that power of expression that made him successful as a public speaker.

After graduating from the University of Georgia, Joseph and his brother John entered the College of Physicians and Surgeons in New York.

When twenty-one years of age, the year before his degree as Doctor of Medicine was conferred, the subject of this sketch made his first noteworthy geological excursion. In his autobiography this prospecting and exploring expedition to the now famous mining district of the south shore of Lake Superior, is dwelt upon with keen pleasure as being the means of leading the young student into the field of science in which he gained distinction. In this expedition, which was the first of its kind, the travelers cruised in boats from the lower lakes to Keewenaw Point, where they had many adventures in the prospectors' camp. From this place Le Conte and his cousin went with the gold hunters and some Indians on a long canoe voyage along the south shore to the present site of Duluth, and thence to the upper waters of the Mississippi and down to the Falls of St. Anthony. The part of the country along which they traveled was entirely uninhabited, and upon the site of the cities of Minneapolis and St. Paul not a cabin was raised.

Dr. Le Conte began the practice of medicine in Macon, Georgia, in 1845. In 1847 he married Caroline Elizabeth Nisbet. They had four children. Two married daughters are now living in Georgia, while a daughter and a son lately married are living in Berkeley with Mrs. Le Conte.

In 1850 attracted by the fame of Agassiz, Le Conte decided, almost within a day, to give up medicine, which had never been a congenial profession to him, and so leaving their newly built home, Mr. and Mrs. Le Conte went to Cambridge, where their second child was born in an old historic house upon the campus of Harvard. This child during subsequent visits to the home of Agassiz, became the playfellow of the great interpreter of nature, and Professor Le Conte used to tell with much amusement of his discovery of the great Agassiz upon his hands and knees, playing horse with the little girl. In 1857, with Agassiz, Dr. Le Conte made a study of the keys and reefs of Florida. Late in this same year, having received the degree of B. S. at Harvard, he returned to Georgia and was elected to the chair of natural science in Ogelthorpe

University. The following year he resigned to accept the chair of geology and natural history in the University of Georgia, in which institution his brother John was the professor of natural philosophy. In 1855 the brothers both resigned their posts and accepted calls to South Carolina College, at Columbia, Joseph to be the professor of geology and natural history and John to be professor of physics. In 1862, the college succombed to the trouble arising out of the Civil War.

In the Journal Professor Le Conte said:—

"During the dark days of the war, I continued to write, 'The Relation of Sociology to Biology,' 'School, College and University,' 'Nature and the Uses of Art.' This was certainly my best. It was written in '63, when the whole South was in an agony of conflict. The college was suspended. I must do something in support of the cause which absorbed every feeling. How could I turn my scientific knowledge to some account? Just then a large manufactory for the production of chemicals for the use of the army was established in the suburbs of Columbia. I was asked to be the chemist. I accepted and for about eighteen months I was engaged in the manufacture on a large scale of many kinds of medicine: alcohol, nitrate of silver, chloroform, sulphuric acid, etc. The whole army drew from this laboratory with the exceptions of those supplies which ran the blockade. In 1864, without solicitation, I was appointed chemist of the Nitre and Mining Bureau, with the rank and pay of Major. My business was to test all nitrous earth brought in from nitre caves or nitre beds. My laboratory was that of the college. I visited all of the caves in South Carolina, Tennessee and Alabama and the iron mines at Shelbyville. I found here a Bessemer furnace, the only one in the Confederate States. I returned to Columbia in September and made my report to St. John, Chief of the Bureau at Richmond. Meanwhile Sherman was coming down from Chattanooga to Atlanta, Johnson in front, retreating step by step. Sherman's march through Georgia is a matter of history. The sea coast of the State was invaded and Savannah surrendered. My second daughter, Mrs. R. M. Davis, was with her aunt within the Federal lines upon my plantation. I felt it my duty to haste to her rescue" * * * Which was accomplished after many difficulties under a flag of truce. They arrived in Columbia February 7, 1865. * * * "I was ahead of Sherman this time, but the army was rapidly approaching. I could hear the guns booming upon the other side of the Congaree River. I now received orders from Colonel St. John to pack up all the chemical apparatus, etc. I sent also all of my valuables, manuscripts, my wife's jewelry, etc. * * *

"Feb. 18, 1864. It was not absolutely certain that Columbia had fallen. We hoped not, or if so, we could not believe that Sherman would deliberately burn it. We had been assured in most positive manner by officers and men of Wheeler's command that there was no enemy in front of us. What was to prevent us then from being cheerful? We were cheerful. The roads, it is true, were still in an awful condition so that we stopped every few hundred yards; but we continued to creep on at the rate of about two miles an hour. But no use in hurrying—no enemy ahead. As usual my brother John. and Captain Green were a little beyond in the buggy. In the glory and brightness of the morning I preferred to walk. My nephew John joined me sometimes and sometimes sat perched high on the trunks and bedding-roll in the wagon. Johnny had been sick and was not stong. The negro women and children were all in the wagons."

These negroes had been brought up from the plantation to work at Columbia in the Nitre Works and, knowing that their freedom had come, chose to go with Professor Le Conte.

"I was walking along rapidly and with a springing step, a little ahead of the wagon. I was just passing a country cabin about a hundred yards from the road. Suddenly I heard, 'Stop, Mister, stop!' I stopped and looking round, saw a country woman rapidly approaching from the house. 'Where are you going!' 'To Allston,' said I. 'To Allston! Don't

you know the Yankees are crossing Broad River not more
than a mile from here? My father is expecting them at our
house every minute!' 'Impossible,' said I. 'We met Wheel-
eɩ's men not more than a mile back and they assured us there
were no Yankees ahead. They ought to know, for they were
sent here to watch them.' 'Wheeler's men!' she retorted,
'don't you see that smoke yonder, and there and there and
yonder!' She pointed rapidly in different directions. I looked,
and to my dismay I saw the rising columns of the smoke of
burning houses on every side, not more than half a mile dis-
tant. We were in the midst of the enemy whom we thought
so far away. Soon the popping of guns, with which I had
become so familiar, commenced. While I was talking with
the woman, John and Captain Green had gotten one-fourth of
a mile ahead.''

Professor Le Conte finally succeeded in warning them and
they concealed themselves and their wagons.

''From our hiding place we saw several parties of Federals
approach the same house during the day. About 11 A. M.
a dense column of smoke, then the squealing of Confederate
pigs and the cackling of Rebel hens and the sound of human
voices in loud and angry tones, proclaimed in unmistakable
language that the hen house nearest us and only 100 yards
from where we were standing, was being raided.''

They remained in hiding all the day. When evening ap-
proached the suspense became great.

''In the meantime the negro children were becoming clamo-
rous for food. They had had nothing since morning. It was
absolutely necessary to make a fire and cook. With many
misgivings and many directions for making it as small as
possible we consented. Alas! Alas! Those crying children,
low whimpering of the hungry mules as fodder was brought
to them and more than all that fire—that dreadful fire—would
surely betray us. As soon as possible it was extinguished
and we went to bed. Anxiety of mind kept us all from sleep
until late. Gradually the hum of the Yankee camp ceased

and all was still as death. I lay awake a long time gazing into the tranquil heavens studded with innumerable stars: and the huge oaks standing like giants with arms uplifted and faces upturned to the sky. Slowly the deep tranquility and holy calm of nature transfused itself into my soul and I sank quietly to sleep."

They were discovered the next morning, but Joseph Le Conte made his escape. His brother John and his nephew were captured.

"I was comparatively safe but my extreme anxiety concerning my brother and nephew rendered it impossible for me to remain quiet. Three or four times in the course of the afternoon, I crept down to the camp; but in every case I found stray Yankees there and had to retreat. My anxiety increased until it became insupportable. * * * I crept down on my hands and knees, closely observing at every step until I came within ten steps of the camp fire. There was no one there but one little negro boy about eight years old. As I rose and walked toward the fire the little fellow started up to run. I called to him to stop and he turned and recognized me."

The negroes greeted Professor Le Conte gladly, told of the capture of his brother and nephew and five negro men. He found that all of his manuscripts had been burned, with all of the silver, jewelry and other articles of personal value. The Confederate supplies had been destroyed also.

The negroes had saved something for their master to eat, after which he sought and found the hiding place of Captain Green.

The hardships endured during the days while Professor Le Conte and Captain Green were making their way to Columbia, are entirely forgotten in his humorous account of their narrow escapes from capture, their ragged condition, and their eagerness to gain rest and food. Captain Green made a good subject for comedy, and the anecdotes told of him are very laughable. Finally they reached their destination:

"We entered Columbia and went down Main street for

a mile and a half. Not a house remaining, only the tall chim-
neys standing gaunt and spectral. The fire had swept five or
six blocks wide right through the heart of the city. We met
not a living soul. Alas, how the beautiful city, the pride of
the State, sat desolate and in ashes!—but I had no time to
moralize. Onward still, with increasing speed. Yonder stood
the brick walls of the college campus and the buildings that
had been saved from the fire to use as a hospital for both
Northern and Southern soldiers. My own ivy-covered home
was seen at last. I resigned the carpet-bag to my companion,
who was to take rooms in the hospital, ran up the stone steps
three at a leap. The door was locked. Rap, rap, rap. Deep
silence a moment, then the quick pattering of little feet along
the hall. Then in an instant open flew the door, and they all
hung upon my neck with mingled laughter and tears. 'Oh,
father, you are soaking wet!' 'You are in rags!' 'Your
pants are hanging in strings about your feet, and look what a
rent in your knees!' ''

All of Professor Le Conte's clothing had been burned, but
the physician at the hospital secured a blue uniform for him,
which, according to the necessity of the time, was worn by
other Confederates.

Though dealing with the last days of the war, when defeat,
disaster, loss of friends and property made many Southerners
very bitter, the journal is utterly free from anything like
strong sectional feeling. The gentleness, sweetness, and hu-
mor of his character is more to be seen in this work than any
other book of Le Conte's. It is filled with illustrations that
are exceedingly comic in their nature, and that indicate the
power for hitting off a humorous situation by pencil sketches
that show how genially the scientist lingered over the laughable memory of awkward hardships, adventures, and the
tricks of accident. Captain Green, in his cloak improvised
from a blanket, makes an especially good subject for a comic
illustration.

During the reconstruction period, the South became almost

unendurable to Southerners of pride. The loss of all of their property and the unfortunate condition of the people was difficult to bear, but the Legislature, composed almost entirely of negroes, voted that negroes should enter the University without any qualifications. At this time the brothers John and Joseph discussed emigrating to Brazil, or considered throwing in their fortunes with those of Maximillian of Mexico. The organization of the University of California, however, brought them to Oakland in 1868. The facts of Professor Le Conte's relation to the University of California are very well known. Of California he writes:

"I have said that my intellectual activity was powerfully stimulated by coming to California. There are many causes for this. First, the reaction from the long agony of the war. Abstract thought was almost impossible during those anxious times and in the presence of its serious results after the war. Second, the splendid field for geological research opened here. Third, contrary to my expectations, I found here an exceptionally active, energetic, and intelligent population. What California wanted then (and still wants to some extent) was a more thoroughly organized society."

Professor and Mrs. Agassiz came to visit the Le Contes in the fall of 1872. Judge Tompkins met the great scientist on this visit, and, through his admiration for the master, established the Agassiz Chair of Oriental Languages.

Professor Le Conte made ten visits to the high Sierras and the Yosemite Valley. The results of these trips have been discussed in his scientific works and in pamphlets, besides the autobiography. He says of his increasing enjoyment in the scenery:

"There is one kind of enjoyment of beauty and grandeur heightened by novelty, and another enjoyment of the same, mellowed and hallowed by association. The one affects more the imagination, the other the heart. I had been so often in the Yosemite that I now loved it for the association of previous delights."

Professor Le Conte's most important discoveries in science are, summed up in the following paragraph, from Professor Lawson's article in *Science :*

"He announced the age and character of the Cascade Mountains and their relation to the great Columbia lava flood; he described the ancient glaciers of the Sierra Nevada, and was among the first to recognize the post-Tertiary elevation of the Sierra Nevada, as shown by the river beds. His studies on mountain structure led him to important generalization on the origin of mountains in general, and he became one of the chief exponents of the 'contractional theory' of mountain building. His studies on ore deposition at Steamboat Springs, Nevada, and Sulphur Bank, California, led him to a discussion of vein formation in general; and his classification of ore deposits has been widely recognized as resting on a sound basis, and is not displaced in its essential features by the most recent attempts in the same direction. He also made important contributions to the subjects of seismology and coral growth in its geological aspects."

Le Conte's important works are called "Sight," "The Elements of Geology," the "Compend of Geology," "Religion and Science," and "Evolution and Its Relation to Religious Thought."

Professor Le Conte was made a member of the National Academy of Sciences, Associate Fellow of the American Academy of Arts and Sciences, corresponding member of the New York Academy of Sciences, member of the American Philosophical Society, Fellow of the American Association for the Advancement of Science and past president of the same, Fellow of the Geological Society of America and past president of the same, life member of the Academy of Sciences, member of the Boston Society of Natural History, honorary member of the Brooklyn Ethical Association, member of the Iowa Academy of Sciences, also of the Davenport Academy of Sciences, member of the American Institute of Mining Engineers, member of the National Geographical Socieiy, member of the International Geological Congress and once vice-president of the same, member of the California State Medical Society, honorary member of the South Carolina State Medical Society. He was also associated with the editorship of the *Journal of Geology and Science.*

Professor Le Conte's articles and books have been translated into other languages, and letters and tributes came to him from all parts of the world. Those expressions of love and veneration that he most appreciated came, however, from his classes. His students were his children, his comrades, and his friends. As one of the fathers of the University, his family is the largest in the State, numbering many hundreds, and these boys and girls speak his name reverently in their homes, where the influence of his cheerful, simple, noble character has made itself felt. He was a great scientist, but a greater man. In his ideal home life and in all of his relations with society he was the courtly gentleman and the charming companion. His book on "Evolution and Its Relation to Religious Thought" has done more toward settling the doubts and calming the troubled souls of the young than many volumes of sermons preached by a less inspired man.

Since '96, the twenty-sixth of February has been celebrated by the students of the University in a way that inadequately expressed their veneration for the great teacher. His long desk was completely covered with flowers, there was always some appropriate gift made to him, and the speech of presentation by a well-known student was always received in a gracious manner by Professor Le Conte. On his last birthday he was in Georgia, and he thought the day would pass unnoticed by the students, but as he was sitting down to his birthday dinner with his wife, his children, his grandchildren, and his great-grandchildren, in his native State, a telegram came from the students of the University of his adopted State, congratulating him upon the rich, complete years of his life. Professor Le Conte was intensely gratified at the arrival of the telegram, but his surprise was great, on reaching Berkeley, to find that the usual gift had been made, in spite of his absence, and a beautiful picture had been sent to his home with the warm greetings of the students. His autobiography closes with an account of this happy home-coming, the final words being :

"Such evidences of affection from the students, the faculty, the regents, and the people of California, have endeared the University and the people to me. There is no place like California."

A TRIBUTE.

BY DARWIN ROOT, '02.

The dear old man has gone and now no more
  The mountains whisper in his listening ear
  The secrets of their inner life. They rear
Their white-crowned heads and scan in vain the shore
Of Time where he has gleaned in years before
  The mysteries of the changing sands, and clear
  And open laid them as a faithful seer
On Truth's broad altar. Now the voice of yore
Is stilled, the face is gone, but ne'er to die
  A memory lives; his voice and face the same
    As in the bygone days may calm our strife,
And e'en in memory may his beaming eye
  E'er dissipate each sordid selfish aim
    And light us to the mountain tops of Life.

The University of California Magazine

(Official Organ of the Alumni Association and of the Council of the Associated Alumni.)

PUBLISHED MONTHLY DURING THE COLLEGE YEAR

Counsellors—PROFESSORS WM. CAREY JONES and THOMAS R. BACON.
Editor-in-Chief—WINFIELD DORN, '02.
Associate Editors—MISS KATHERINE F. SMITH, '02; MISS LUCILE GRAVES, '03; ROBT. W. RITCHIE, '02; BENJ. W. REED, '02; JOHN A. BREWER, 'C3; ROGER C. CHICKERING, '04, J. RAYMOND CARTER, '02 (Staff Artist).
Alumni Contributors—PROFESSOR WM. E. RITTER President of the Associated Alumni; CHARLES S. GREENE, President of the Alumni Association; MISS EMMA HEFTY, Secretary of the Associated Alumni; JAMES SUTTON, Secretary of the Alumni Association.
Business Manager—BRYAN BELL, '03,

[The subscription price of the magazine is $1 50 per year, payable in advance. Failure of the managers to receive a notice from subscribers to discontinue sending the publication will be taken as an intimation that the subscription is to be continued. Advertising rates will be sent on application to the manager, Berkeley, Cal.]

The Magazine is on sale at the Coöperative Store, University; Needham Brothers,' Berkeley; Elder & Shepard, 238 Post St., San Francisco.
Patrons will please note the new San Francisco address.
Student'subscribers will receive their copies at the Coöperative Store until further notice.

WE stand silent before the swish of the scythe of Time. A life has gone out of our midst for which nothing can compensate. How much the influence, the personality, the sacrifice, of Joseph Le Conte has contributed to the University can never be measured by material or intellectual standards. It reaches as deep as feeling and as high as thought.

Life hurries on,—but the influence of a great personality is for eternity. Unconsciously we are feeling the permeating influence of the life of Joseph Le Conte,—and this spirit will

ts on the Glycogenic function of the Liver and its rela-
ital force and vital heat; by JOSEPH LeCONTE.

the National Academy of Sciences, New York, October, 1877.]

t size of the liver and its persistence as a conspicu-
s we go down the animal scale even to a very low
arly demonstrate the great importance of its func-
conclusion is entirely confirmed by the very grave
e health produced by its disorders. But in spite of
dged importance, great obscurity still hangs about
ure of its functions. The function of the liver is
like that of the lungs or the kidneys, but very
The liver is the manufactory of both bile and sugar.
both a *secretion* used in the digestive preparation
l an *excretion*, separating poisonous matters from
The sugar, too, has doubtless as many and as complex uses; but these are little understood. Evidently, therefore, any light, even the smallest, thrown upon this sugar-mak-
ing function of the liver will be hailed with pleasure both by
the scientific physiologist and by the medical practitioner.

What I have to offer on this subject, however, is not the result of any elaborate research, nor of the discovery of any new
facts, but simply the result of thought on, and necessary de-
duction from, facts already known. Neither are all the
thoughts and deductions entirely new, but I cannot find that
they have been held sufficiently firmly and stated sufficiently
clearly by physiological writers, and for this reason, perhaps,
have not borne any fruit in medical practice.

It will not be amiss to review very briefly the main and
usually acknowledged facts connected with this function.

1. The portal blood of *flesh-fed* animals contains no sugar,
but the same blood, after passing through the liver, i. e., the
blood of the hepatic vein, contains always a notable quan-
tity of this substance. Evidently, therefore, *it is manufactured
in the liver.*

2. If the dead liver removed from the body be washed out
completely by water injected through the portal and hepatic
veins until every trace of sugar is removed, and then the liver
be allowed to stand a while, on recommencing the transmission
of water the first that passes is decidedly sugary. The same process may be repeated several times with the same result, until
the material out of which the sugar is made is finally exhausted.

3. If the liver of any animal be kept a considerable time
before cooking, the amount of sugar which accumulates in its

Lightning Source UK Ltd.
Milton Keynes UK
UKHW022204021218
333278UK00006B/639/P